Letter to the Church at Ephesus

FIRST LOVE & FIRST WORKS

Christ's principles for keeping covenant

relationship

Dr. Austin de Bourg

ISBN-10: 1546445633

ISBN-13: 978-1546445630

Library of Congress Control Number: 2017907253

CreateSpace Independent Publishing Platform,

North Charleston, South Carolina

TABLE OF CONTENTS

PART II: FIRST WORKS

ACKNOWLEDGMENT

I wish to acknowledge members of my staff, Maria Parris, Toni Kimbrough and Michaella Frederick, for their labor of love in the compilation and editing of this book; and for searching through the manuscript for any type of errors they could find, and the areas they felt needed more clarity. Together, through their godly maturity and analytical minds, they proved to be invaluable contributors to the final product.

FOREWORD

I have a limitless capacity for detail, a need to dissect a thing, an idea, into its minutest parts in order to grasp, to its fullest, what is being imparted. It is no wonder that my All-Knowing Heavenly Father has found it fit to have me sit under the ministry of Apostle Dr. Austin J. de Bourg, one of God's greatest revelators of the heart, mind and ways of God. His revelatory writings flow out of His years of personal experiences with the Lord, His personal teacher and mentor. Furthermore, he shares from a heartfelt desire for others to experience that intimacy with the Lord which he has come to enjoy, and so he gives us realism and genuineness with simplicity. Long troubling questions are answered bringing understanding and fulfilment in the Lord. I feel sure that as you read this, and other of his writings, you too would be richer for the why's and how's of God and of your Christian walk.

This new book by Dr. Austin de Bourg, *Letter to the Church at Ephesus: First Love and First Works,* will certainly confirm the above. There is a depth and clarity of revelation that would rekindle a holy fear and a passion in you to ensure that you secure your eternity with God. So clear is the revelation that one's eternity is intricately tied to *first love* and *first works,* that I believe no one will miss just how vital these two principles are to their Christian walk. Furthermore, one will not be able to overlook the pathway to God's infinite blessings which is precisely enunciated in this book. We go about our Christian lives hoping for God's blessings, yet not being aware that these blessings are so intrinsically tied to our relationship with our fellow brothers and sisters in Christ. I mean, who would ever think that God's blessings are tied to the extent of our joining with one another. What an eye-opener! Moreover, the how's and why's are plainly laid out so that a heart that is earnest will not miss the Lord.

The chapter on Covenant truly stood out for me. I came into a fresh understanding of the binding connection that is rooted in *first love* with Jesus Christ and was able to grasp the marvelous obligations inherent in that joining to Him. I am encouraged to stay abiding in the "vine" so that I may reap the benefits of the caring and preserving power so intrinsic to being in relationship with Him. I know that you would be encouraged to do the same.

The smoothness of the flow in his writing and the build-up of the points which together unveil these necessary truths are astounding. The accounts offered are precise and without superfluous details. Excellent!! The references are rightly positioned so as not to interrupt the flow, and the short commentaries that lead us into the scriptures are so full of insight. But best of all, as you read, the atmosphere that would pervade would be filled with the Lord's persuasion and a drawing into Him that is so characteristic of intimacy with Him. I assure you that you will have to stop at several points to just wallow in His Presence for a while!

Althea Bastien

PREFACE

This book is the first of an expository series on the letters which Jesus Christ wrote to the seven Churches in the Book of Revelation, chapters two and three. This seven-part series underscores a shocking fact revealed in these letters, and that is . . . *how wrong church leaders and their congregations could be about their position in God, all the while thinking that they are in His perfect will and in right standing with Him.*

My intention is for these books to be a *major* eye opener for those who truly want to be in the will of God, as this is indeed so absolutely vital to Christians individually and corporately.

Each volume delves into a particular letter, providing a revelatory study of Jesus' counsel. In these letters, Jesus specifically details where each Church went wrong, clearly identifying the errors wrought by their misguided presumption, and prescribes the corrective direction as the Head and

Chief Apostle of *His Church.* Hence, He gave them the opportunity to correct their wrong thinking and faulty expectations of what would qualify them for heaven.

While each Church represents a certain period in Church history, and each had a specific purpose, God's general principles and requirements are unchanging and applicable to His Church in every Church age. This study will reveal just how relevant these letters are today, and that they could well be the **very thing that is needed to put this current-day Church of Jesus Christ on the right course.**

As we focus on these seven letters, a very sobering truth emerges and that is that though most of these seven historical Churches had many, varied and great achievements, and had received Jesus Christ's due commendation, still **five of the seven Churches were, in fact, in a fallen state and, therefore, did not qualify to maintain their place in the body of Christ.** Furthermore, we see that these fallen Churches were not even aware that they were fallen and, in fact, thought they were right with God. Imagine the shock it must have been for them to learn their true state. We are indeed at a great disadvantage when we are fallen but do not know that we are.

These books will help you to safeguard yourself from falling into this predicament. They present revelation and insights into these seven letters with simplicity and clarity so that you can fully grasp their significance. It is my hope that through these writings, you would be challenged to re-examine your own position with God and take the corrective steps to be in His will.

As you read through the pages of this teaching series, you will learn how to apply those things which Jesus Christ prescribed to the fallen Churches to your own lives. You will uncover the keys to maintaining covenant relationship with Jesus Christ and with one another, which is so critical in securing your salvation and entrance into heaven. Furthermore, you will discover that right relationship with the Trinity, both personal and corporate, is the only way through which real love, faith and obedience could be fostered. These are the true requirements for making it into heaven, and not the labor, toil and useless sacrifices in which many have put their faith.

Read these books with an open heart and you will find, hidden within these simple writings, the secret to entering into an **intimate** relationship with Jesus Christ, God the Father, and the Holy Spirit. It is my hope that, as you read, you will come to realize an important truth, which is, that settling for just being saved and content to do good works, without actively maintaining this intimate relationship with the Trinity, would not guarantee you a place in the Body of Christ and in the kingdom of Heaven.

Study these books with a desire to receive that same *Spirit of Truth* through Whom Jesus Christ gave the corrective commands to the seven Churches to get them on the path that leads to God's perfect will. I have written them out of obedience to my Lord and Savior Jesus Christ and His divine call to me to restore lost Biblical Truths and Biblical Christianity.

It is my sincere hope that they will imprint upon your hearts the seriousness of living this Christian life, based first and foremost on relationship and not on natural accomplishments.

I pray that this exposition will encourage you to diligently seek to remain in right standing with Jesus Christ, the Father and the Holy Spirit, for the alternative is unthinkable: on that day of judgement, when you are fully expecting to hear, "well done, thou good and faithful servant," (Matthew 25:21) but instead you hear, "depart from me, ye that work iniquity!" (Matthew 7:23). I urge you therefore, to soberly consider the teachings contained in this series and live up to your foremost purpose of being "in Christ," so that when that time comes you will not be disqualified.

That day may come so suddenly, that it would be too late to recover, should you be in a fallen condition. Therefore, I exhort you, as the word of God does, to let *today* be the day of salvation, for tomorrow may be too late.

. . . behold, now is the accepted time; behold,
now is the day of salvation.

—2 Corinthians 6:2b

Austin J. de Bourg

INTRODUCTION

The apostle John was on the isle of Patmos when he heard a voice speak with such authority that he was compelled to turn towards it. Standing before John was Jesus Christ, clothed in glorious magnificence, in the midst of seven golden candlesticks, and in His hands were seven stars. John, upon seeing Him, fell "as dead" at His feet.[1] Jesus explained this mysterious scene to John, saying:

> The mystery of the seven stars which thou sawest in my right hand, and the seven golden candlesticks. The seven stars are the angels of the seven churches: and **the seven candlesticks which thou sawest are the seven churches.**
>
> —Revelation 1:20 (emphasis added)

Jesus had been carefully observing each of these churches and evaluating their readiness for His return . . . that day when He will come, not as Savior,

---

[1] Revelation 1:1–19

but as Lord and King. Through the hand of His servant, the apostle John, Jesus issued letters to each church, leaving for us a record of His appraisal and the somber counsel that He issued, not just to His Church of that era, but to His Church throughout the ages so that there would be no doubt about His expectations.

Though each of these seven letters is of importance to us, this exposition, *First Love and First Works,* focuses on the letter addressed to the Church at Ephesus. I invite you, therefore, to look with me more closely at the Lord's letter to the Ephesians.

Being a just Lord, Jesus commends the church for all those things that He has found to be praise-worthy:

> I know thy works, and thy labour, and thy patience, and how thou canst not bear them which are evil: and thou hast tried them which say they are apostles, and are not, and hast found them liars: [3] And hast borne, and hast patience, and for my name's sake hast

laboured, and hast not fainted.

—Revelation 2:2–3 (emphasis added)

What admirable commendations! This church was well known for its uncompromising commitment to uphold the truth of God's word. They had been schooled through the years by such outstanding teachers as the apostle Paul, Timothy and, later on, by the apostle John. With such distinguished instructors, it is no wonder that the Ephesians were well established in godly doctrine and were quick to discern and denounce those who preached anything contrary to truth. Additionally, no one could fault this church for their evangelistic zeal, their commitment to prayer, and their many good works. What a wonderful church! Surely, the Lord must be pleased!

God's perspective, however, is often quite different to man's. The Lord's requirement for His people and His Church goes beyond good works, as wonderful and necessary as these are, and this is why Jesus delivered an ominous warning to the Ephesians:

> Nevertheless I have somewhat against thee, because **thou hast left thy first love.**[5] Remember therefore from whence thou art fallen, and repent, and **do the first works**; or else I will come unto thee quickly, and will remove thy candlestick out of his place, except thou repent."
>
> —Revelation 2:4–5 (emphasis added)

Jesus declared that this church had left their "***first love***" and that they had failed to do "**the *first works*.**" In His view, they had "fallen," which is to say, they were in a backslidden place, and were in danger of having their "candlestick" removed. Unless they repented and began to demonstrate *first love* and to do the *first works,* they would be forever disconnected from His Church—His body of believers. Imagine the shock on the faces of the members of the Ephesian church when they read these words! Where did this *first love* and *first works* come from and why did they seem to matter so much to Jesus?

Many believe that *first love* and *first works* are the same but they are not. Jesus admonished the church at Ephesus that they, having left, must **return** to their *first love* and **do** the *first works*. Clearly then, these are two distinct, albeit intricately connected concepts. This will become clearer as we delve into our study.

The terms *first love* and *first works* appear only in the very last book of the Bible, the book of Revelation, chapter two verses four and five. As such, many Christians today may question and even dismiss their significance. However, as this discourse will unveil, they are vital, fundamental principles in which one's eternal destiny is wrapped. My intention in this book is to guide the reader through the scriptures, placing "precept upon precept" and "line upon line" as God instructs us to do as we study His Word[2], so that we may comprehend the eternal significance that God has always placed on *first love*

---

[2] "Whom shall he teach knowledge? and whom shall he make to understand doctrine? them that are weaned from the milk, and drawn from the breasts. [10] For precept must be upon precept, precept upon precept; line upon line, line upon line; here a little, and there a little:"—Isaiah 28:9–10

and *first works.* We will see that these doctrines are woven consistently throughout the Bible for our benefit, underpinning their enduring importance to God.

Jesus' additional warning to the Church at Ephesus further underscores the irrefutable weight of *first love* and the *first works* to God:

> He that hath an ear, let him hear what the Spirit saith unto the churches; **To him that overcometh will I give to eat of the tree of life,** which is in the midst of the paradise of God.
>
> —Revelation 2:7 (emphasis added)

God's Word makes it abundantly clear that *first love* and *first works* are determining factors as to whether or not we will "eat of the tree of life" and live forever in the kingdom of Heaven. The alternative is unthinkable . . . spiritual death—separation from God for all eternity!

I invite you, therefore, to join me in exploring the undeniable power of *first love* and *first works.*

PART I: FIRST LOVE

Nevertheless I have somewhat against thee, because
thou hast left thy first love.

—Revelation 2:4 (emphasis added)

CHAPTER 1

WHAT IS FIRST LOVE?

———◆❖◆———

Firgt love is that love which expresses the deepest affection and devotion for a particular person, a love that supersedes the affection and devotion for any other.

Let us explore this concept of *first love* to discover why it is of such significance to Jesus Christ and why its neglect should attract such dire consequence (Revelation 2:4–5). We see in the gospels that Jesus speaks of a **"first"** commandment to which His Church must adhere:

> And thou shall love the Lord thy God with all thy heart, and with all thy soul, and with all thy mind, and with all thy strength: this is the **first commandment.**
>
> —Mark 12:30 (emphasis added)

This commandment declares that we must love God with all our being and that our love for Him must be first and foremost in our hearts and minds. This forms the basis for the concept of **first love,** to which Jesus referred. Let us now examine the term *first love* in greater detail.

First love is derived from the Greek words, "protos agape." "**Protos,**" meaning "first" speaks of that which is foremost in time or place: first in honor, in influence, in rank, and in importance.[3] The word "***agape***" is translated into our English word, "love" and is used to speak of affection, good will, benevolence, brotherly love, and charity.[4] None of these words in English, however, adequately captures the depth of the original Greek word, *agape,* which is used in the scriptures to describe the God kind of love—a love that is pure, sacrificial, unconditional and unchanging.

---

[3] "G4413 - prōtos - Strong's Greek Lexicon (KJV)." Blue Letter Bible. Web. 5 March, 2017.
[4] "G26 - agapē - Strong's Greek Lexicon (KJV)." Blue Letter Bible. Web. 5 March, 2017.

Based on Jesus' commandment to love God, and taking into consideration this expanded definition of *first love—protos agape—*we can conclude that the *"first love"* to which Jesus was referring is that **unwavering love (agape) which believers in Christ ought to reserve in their hearts for the Father, Jesus Christ and the Holy Spirit, placing the Trinity above everyone and everything, and giving God *first place*—that supreme place of honor, affection and importance in their lives.**

It is important for believers to understand that *first love* is not an empty declaration but it is the response of a heart that has been redeemed by the love of the Father, expressed through the sacrifice of His Son, Jesus Christ:

> For God so loved the world, that he gave his only begotten Son, that whosoever believeth in him should not perish, but have everlasting life.
>
> —John 3:16

Our natural response to such an extraordinary love should be to love in return out of loyalty and gratitude for all that Jesus Christ and the Father have done and are still doing for us. Those who relate to Him from *first love* will even lay down their lives for Jesus Christ as the early Christians did. This *first love* relationship preserved and expanded the Christian faith, demonstrating its invincibility.

When we have *first love* for God we will **cleave** to Him and seek only to please him by doing His will. This word "cleave" speaks of being firmly adhered, as if with glue; of abiding or pursuing hard after a person or thing.[5] This is the way we ought to be with Jesus Christ and with God the Father, having that fixed determination to maintain unbroken fellowship with Them, allowing nothing and no one to separate us from Them.

---

[5] The word "cleave" is derived from the Hebrew word **"dabaq"** meaning: "to adhere especially firmly as if with glue; to be glued"; "abide fast, follow close (hard after), be joined together" ["H1692 - dabaq - Strong's Hebrew Lexicon (KJV)." Blue Letter Bible. Web. 3 March, 2017.]

From the very beginning and down through the ages, God has yearned for this *first love* from His people. We see this thread running consistently throughout the scriptures from Genesis to Revelation.

CHAPTER 2

FIRST LOVE:
FROM GENESIS TO REVELATION

⎯⎯⎯◈⎯⎯⎯

Everything that God conceives is a **perfect prototype** or pattern to which He intends His children to adhere with great care. This principle of *first love* is one such prototype, and was established with Adam and Eve at the very dawn of man's history on the earth. Let us now go to the Garden of Eden where we will see this principle unfold as we discover God's intent and purpose for mankind in this regard.

When God fashioned Adam and Eve, He created them primarily for intimate relationship and fellowship with Him and, subsequently, with each other. He lavished His love upon them as a Father would upon his beloved children. Of all created beings, man held first place in God's heart.

Adam was created first as God tenderly and brilliantly formed his body from the dust. God also did the unprecedented. He placed within Adam a spirit like His own and breathed His essence . . . His very own breath . . . into Adam, pouring life, love, and light into man. This earthly son of God was made in the image of His Creator—bearing His very nature and characteristics and, therefore, Adam could do what no other created being could do. He could commune with God at the deepest level . . . spirit to Spirit—like communing with Like—and enjoy wonderful, intimate relationship with his Creator, his God and his Father. This *first love* relationship has always been God's desire for man.

Then, out of Adam's side, God fashioned for His son the woman, Eve. She was Adam's "help meet" (Genesis 2:18), his **ezer**[6] **kenegdo**[7] [8],

---

[6] "H5828 - `ezer - Strong's Hebrew Lexicon (KJV)." Blue Letter Bible. Web. 19 March, 2017.
The word **ezer** is defined as *"succor, or support."* and Gesenius' Hebrew-Chaldee Lexicon states that *"the primary idea lies in girding, surrounding, hence defending."*

his counterpart, given to him as a support to encourage and defend him. Joined to each other, they were to mirror Christ's nature, strengthen each other and guard and uphold God's purposes above all else.

God's deepest desire was that together, Adam and Eve would instinctively respond to His love by retaining for Him a place in their hearts that would be rivalled by nothing and by no one. His hope was that they would *cleave* to Him with unwavering love and affection—with *protos agape*—that love that exceeds the bond of every other relationship. Adam and Eve were God's children—His family—created to love. As their heavenly Father would lavish His pure love upon them, demonstrating this love explicitly, personally, and intimately, Adam and Eve, in turn, would pour that love back onto Him. As long as Adam and Eve cleaved to God and

---

[7] Alexander, Ralph H. "Marriage." Baker's Evangelical Dictionary of Biblical Theology, edited by Walter A. Elwell, Baker Books, 1996. *Bible Study Tools Online*.

[8] Faston, M.G. "Help-meet." Illustrated Bible Dictionary, Cosimo, 2005. *Bible Study Tools Online*.

followed His laws and instructions, giving Him first place in their lives, they lived by this all-important, primary principle of *first love*, and thus, they pleased God.

Unfortunately, there came a time when Adam and Eve disobeyed God's command. They partook of the tree of *Knowledge of Good and Evil* of which He forbade them to partake. Thus, sin was first conceived. Sin is disobedience to God's word. Adam and Eve, in disobeying God had violated the principle of *first love*.

Scripture records that Satan had come to Eve in the Garden of Eden in the form of a serpent insinuating that God was withholding something good from them and suggested to Eve that if they listened to him instead of God, they too would become as gods. Eve, allowing herself to be enticed by Satan, fell for his lie, then she convinced Adam to disobey God's command and also eat from the tree of which He had expressly forbidden them to eat. Adam and Eve had made a decision to listen to the words of another—and a lesser being at that. God took their decision seriously because they had stepped out of the place of *first love* and away from God's protective covering, leaving themselves exposed to Satan's bombardment of their natural senses.

Ever since the Garden, God's deep longing for *first love* from His children has never waned and is etched within the pages of scripture. Listen to God as He speaks to His chosen people, the children of Israel in the Book of Deuteronomy:

> That thou mayest **love the LORD thy God**, *and* that thou mayest **obey his voice**, and that thou mayest **cleave** unto him: for he *is* thy life, and the length of thy days: that thou mayest dwell in the land which the LORD sware unto thy fathers, to Abraham, to Isaac, and to Jacob, to give them.
> —Deuteronomy 30:20 (emphasis added)

Though written centuries after Adam and Eve, this verse of scripture points to the unbroken communion which God had, from the very beginning, purposed to be the inherent sustaining factor of man's existence. It reveals that God wants His children to cleave to Him, not from a sense of obligation, but out of a heart which treasures and responds to the great gift of His love.

This principle of *first love* was reiterated when God gave His people specific laws to adhere to so that they would remain in right standing and in fellowship with Him. His very first commandment to them encapsulated the principle of *first love*:

> **Thou shalt have no other gods before me.** [4] Thou shalt not make unto thee any graven image, or any likeness of anything that is in heaven above, or that is in the earth beneath, or that is in the water under the earth. [5] **Thou shalt not bow down thyself to them, nor serve them: for** I **the** Lord **thy God am a jealous God,** visiting the iniquity of the fathers

upon the children unto the third and fourth generation of them that hate me; ⁶ And shewing mercy unto thousands of them that love me, and keep my commandments.

—Exodus 20:3–6 (emphasis added)

The call to *first love* resonates throughout the bible over and over again. Every godly leader and every prophet of God recorded in scripture urged God's people toward *first love*. Listen, for example, to Joshua as He addressed God's people:

But take diligent heed to do the commandment and the law, which Moses the servant of the Lord charged you, **to love the Lord your God, and to walk in all his ways, and to keep his commandments, and to cleave unto him, and to serve him with all your heart and with all your soul.**

—Joshua 22:5 (emphasis added)

The Bible tells us that God is a jealous God, not in some distorted or selfish way, but because He loves us and He knows that when we fall from our *first love*, we become disconnected from Him, the One who is the source of our life-function and of every blessing . . . spiritual, physical, emotional and mental wellness; divine provision and protection. It is because God loved His people and desired to protect them always that He admonished them to guard against anything or anyone who might entice them away from this life-giving and life-sustaining relationship.

It is no wonder that God was always grieved when the devotion of His children towards Him was replaced by their religion. Consider, for instance, God's opening statements in the Book of Isaiah. Speaking through His prophet, God passionately expresses His intense sorrow over those who had shifted their focus and devotion from Him to their religious rituals and traditions:

Hear, O heavens, and give ear, O earth: for the Lord hath spoken, **I have**

nourished and brought up children,
and they have rebelled against me.
³ The ox knoweth his owner, and the ass
his master's crib: but Israel doth not
know, my people doth not consider. ⁴ Ah
sinful nation, a people laden with
iniquity, a seed of evildoers, children that
are corrupters: **they have forsaken
the Lord, they have provoked the Holy
One of Israel unto anger, they are gone
away backward.**

—Isaiah 1: 2–4 (emphasis added)

God had poured His love upon His
children—the chosen people, Israel—and had
protected and provided for them supernaturally,
blessing them in every way. He had brought them
into covenant relationship with Himself and thus,
He favored them above all the nations. In spite of
all that He had done to show them His deep love
and His faithfulness toward them, the people had
become complacent and indifferent toward Him.
They had left their *first love*. Their hearts had
grown apathetic toward God even though they
continued to religiously offer the established

sacrifices, perform the required rituals, and were meticulous in keeping their religious feast days. Listen to God's heart:

> To what purpose is the multitude of your sacrifices unto me? saith the LORD: I am full of the burnt offerings of rams, and the fat of fed beasts; and I delight not in the blood of bullocks, or of lambs, or of he goats. [12] When ye come to appear before me, who hath required this at your hand, to tread my courts? [13] Bring no more vain oblations; incense is an abomination unto me; the new moons and sabbaths, the calling of assemblies, I cannot away with; it is iniquity, even the solemn meeting. [14] Your new moons and your appointed feasts my soul hateth: they are a trouble unto me; I am weary to bear them.
>
> —Isaiah 1:11–14

The people had mistakenly assumed that these religious practices would satisfy God, yet from His response we see that they had missed their true purpose . . . relationship! They no longer held God in *first love* and were oblivious of the fact that they were out of His will and thus had removed themselves from His divine covering and protection. As a nation they were now exposed, spiritually and physically to the ravages of sins' consequences:

> . . . the whole head is sick, and the whole heart faint. [6] From the sole of the foot even unto the head there is no soundness in it; but wounds, and bruises, and putrifying sores: they have not been closed, neither bound up, neither mollified with ointment. [7] Your country is desolate, your cities are burned with fire: your land, strangers devour it in your presence, and it is desolate, as overthrown by strangers. [8] And the daughter of Zion is left as a cottage in a vineyard, as a lodge in a garden of cucumbers, as a besieged city. [9] Except the Lord of hosts had left unto us a very small remnant, we should have been as Sodom, and we should have been like unto Gomorrah.
>
> —Isaiah 1:5b–9

The Jews, as a result of turning their focus away from God, suffered not only personal affliction but also their entire country had become "desolate" and "besieged" by enemy forces. God had allowed these consequences of their error so that they would repent and return to Him, yet not even their dire state seemed to awaken them to their true condition. Even though time and time again, God, who is loving, merciful, compassionate, and long-suffering, had attempted to draw His people back to *first love* for Him, they did not heed his appeals.

Permit me to mention, that it is indeed alarming that when Christians today sometimes suffer through unrelenting sickness, poverty, loss of resources, and all manner of trouble, they do not seem to even consider that perhaps it is so because they have left their *first love*. Yet, it is clear that their lifestyles do not reflect their relationship with Jesus Christ and God the Father as the ultimate and infinite purpose for their lives. Sadly, many Christians today do not uphold this undergirding principle of *first love* but instead focus primarily on themselves, on religious duties, and on the pursuit of worldliness. Many fail to realize that in spite of any worldly achievements or commendations they may gain, if their first priority is not centered on maintaining *first love* for Jesus Christ and God the Father, they set themselves up to be expelled from the body of Christ and the Church of Jesus Christ, and consequently open themselves to all manner of sickness and trouble.

This principle of *first love* continues in the New Testament. Jesus and His apostles taught about it and lived it as recorded throughout the gospels and epistles. Additionally, many of the New Testament saints gave their lives willingly rather than give up their *first love* for Jesus Christ.

I tell you, the call to *first love* is not a new thing! It has pulsed in God's heart through every age and, in His eyes, nothing is more important. Today, God continues to draw His children back to *first love* for Him but many are too caught up in other matters to even hear, far less respond to

God's call to return to Him and put Him first. We can be sure however, that if *first love* for Jesus Christ is absent in Christians today, then we too, like the Israelites, may unexpectedly find ourselves in the same tragic position with our countries "besieged" by demonic and controlling forces that would work against us. This is because we have removed ourselves, our families and our nations from God's divine covering. The Church today must hear and respond to Christ's call to *first love*; our eternal state depends upon it.

CHAPTER 3

OBEDIENCE: PROOF OF FIRST LOVE

"If ye love me, keep my commandments."
—John 14:15

These are the words of Jesus Christ to His disciples. Obedience to Him and His word is an undeniable and primary proof of *first love* (John 14:21). We cannot therefore claim to love Jesus Christ and yet persist in disobedience to His word and His will. This *first love* obedience however, is not merely an outward, ritualistic act but it is an obedience forged through sustained relationship done willingly in reciprocation of Christ's love for us.

At every step of His journey on earth, Jesus remained obedient to God, thus demonstrating *first love* toward His Father, and rejected Satan's constant attempts to lure Him away from God's purposes and His ways. Neither wealth nor glory, and not even intense physical need, could move Jesus from *first love* for His Father. You see, **first love will not allow us to fall in love with temporal things like money, fame and glory.** Neither would distress, disappointment or despair displace Jesus Christ in our hearts. In fact, *first love* will even cause us to accept suffering, if need be, to fulfill the Father's desire and will, declaring just as Jesus did when confronted with the dreadful reality of the cross, ". . . nevertheless not my will, but thine, be done." (Luke 22:42b).

As we saw in the account of Adam and Eve above, it was their disobedience to God that caused them to step out of *first love.* Neither Adam nor Eve recognized the underlying deception of Satan's suggestion. By Eve's disobedience to God's command, she inadvertently dishonored God and disregarded the supremacy and integrity of His word. As for Adam, instead of functioning as the leader that God had made him to be, he naively allowed Eve to assume the leadership position and yielded to her satanic counsel. By doing so, he too disobeyed

God and broke his *first love* relationship with God.

By their disobedience, Adam and Eve had unwittingly rejected communion with God, treating that most precious gift recklessly, and they paid a terrible price for it . . . they were cast out from Eden and from God's presence, forfeiting their privilege as sons of God.

> Therefore the Lord God sent him forth from the garden of Eden, to till the ground from whence he was taken. [24] So he drove out the man; and he placed at the east of the garden of Eden Cherubims, and a flaming sword which turned every way, to keep the way of the tree of life.
>
> —Genesis 3:23–24

When we choose to operate in the principle of *first love*, we are affirming that God is worthy of our deepest love, honor, and respect, and, as such, we make a determination not to usurp His place in our hearts or reject His loving authority over our lives by being disobedient to His word and His will. *First love* will oppose the very thought of willfully offending Jesus Christ. We will gladly remain faithful to Jesus Christ and to His word, regardless of circumstance or feelings. If we have *first love* in our hearts, we would not heed any counsel that is contrary to His word, irrespective of who may be the counselor— religious leader or opposer.

CHAPTER 4

FIRST LOVE: IN SUMMARY

———◆———

If we look now at the Church at Ephesus against this fresh perspective of *first love,* we can understand why the Lord rebuked them so strongly and threatened to remove their "candlestick." The opinion of the Church at Ephesus, was that their accomplishments had placed them in good standing with Jesus Christ and with God the Father. Nevertheless, Jesus' letter to them reveals His and the Father's perspective and Their interpretation of the Church's success and failure. The Ephesians must have been stunned to hear that they were in a fallen state in spite of their many accomplishments. This should be an important lesson for every Christian and every assembly: that if, in the process of laboring untiringly to sustain and advance the cause of Christ, we place more importance on the labor and accomplishments than on maintaining our *first love* for Jesus Christ, we too, like the Church at Ephesus, are in a fallen state.

Loss of intimate love for Jesus Christ is sometimes masked by good ideas, good programs, and good deeds. As far as Jesus Christ and God the Father are concerned, without *first love*, these amount to nothing more than deceptive presumption. Anyone who thinks that good deeds and religion could earn them a place in the kingdom of God and heaven is deceived and is sorely lacking in the knowledge of God and His purpose for their life. Without *first love* for Jesus Christ, their good deeds and their religious rituals are nothing more than "self" wanting to determine its own way of living as opposed to embracing God's way. God views this as rebellion and does not align Himself with it because it seeks to replace what Jesus Christ did in order that man would have the opportunity to come back to God. Acts of benevolence are pleasing and acceptable to God, but it is not profitable to us if our benevolence displaces our *first love*, our affection and devotion toward Him. The admonition of Christ to the Church at Ephesus bears this out: "thou hast left thy first love. . . repent, and do the first works; or else I will come unto thee quickly, and will remove thy candlestick out of his place, except thou repent." which, being paraphrased, says, "you would lose your place in the body of Christ and in the kingdom of God."

From Genesis to Revelation, the message is the same. When man loses his *first love* for Jesus Christ and God, he removes himself from God's Presence, divine covering and blessings. He is in a fallen state. However, because of the finished work of Jesus Christ, he has the opportunity to repent of his sin, renew his love, faith, and obedience to Jesus Christ and thereby recover from the fall.

PART II: FIRST WORKS

Remember therefore from whence thou art fallen, and repent, and **do the first works;**

—Rev 2:5a (emphasis added)

CHAPTER 5

THE FUNDAMENTALS OF FIRST WORKS

H aving established what *first love* is, let us now explore the *first works* which Jesus commands us to *do* so that we might understand why it too holds eternal implications for us.

Defining First Works

The "*first works*" is the terminology that Jesus Christ used to describe the practice of all the principles He instituted to govern the Christian faith. The use of the word "works" in *first works* does not refer to labor or toil as it is commonly used. In context, it refers to the **primary or foremost occupational responsibility and behavior of each believer in Christ,** that is, believers are responsible for upholding the welfare of one another, out of love for one another, for the purpose of keeping covenant relationship. Thus Jesus instituted the *first works* as the key component in our living out the godly principles and practices intended to keep us united in love, communion, and fellowship. **Precisely put, the *first works* are the observable evidence of Christians' covenant relationship with Jesus Christ and with one another.**

In keeping with the standard practice of covenant relationships, when the two parties join in covenant, they become one.[9] So too, when we enter into covenant relationship with Christ and with one another we are no longer separate, distinct individuals operating on our own but we become one with Christ and with one another in spirit. We find a new identity in Christ . . . a more powerful and wondrous identity. This new identity is the Body of Christ—the family of God—and if we are to honor our covenant with Christ, we must put aside our individualism, and love for Him and for His Body must take pre-eminence over our feelings and individual ideas

---

[9] See chapter 8 on Covenant Relationship.

and plans. In this, *first love* for Jesus Christ is reflected and by upholding the principles that constitute the *first works*, we qualify to be part of the body of Christ. Listen to Jesus' prayer for His Body:

> Neither pray I for these alone, but for them also which shall believe on me through their word; [21] **That they all may be one; as thou, Father, art in me, and I in thee**, that they also may be one in us: that the world may believe that thou hast sent me. [22] And the glory which thou gavest me I have given them; **that they may be one, even as we are one:** [23] **I in them, and thou in me, that they may be made perfect in one**; and that the world may know that thou hast sent me, and hast loved them, as thou hast loved me.
> —John 17:20–23 (emphasis added)

The Bible tells us that each of us is considered as **one member** of the body of Christ. It is **together** that we form the whole body of Christ, Jesus Himself being the Head, the One who directs the body.

> So we, being many, are one body **in Christ**, and every one members one of another.
>
> —Romans 12:5 (emphasis added)

> For as the body is one, and hath many members, and all the members of that one body, being many, are one body: so also is Christ. [13] For by one Spirit are we all baptized into one body, whether we be Jews or Gentiles, whether we be bond or free; and have been all made to drink into one Spirit. [14] For the body is not one member, but many.
>
> —1 Corinthians 12:12–14

First works enable the proper functioning of the body of Christ and assist in maintaining its invincibility. This is what made the early Church invincible and it is that very thing which will make today's Church invincible.

Without question, **the early apostles understood the significance and sustaining power of the *first works* and they continually pointed the Church toward it.** It is to the benefit of Christians today to ensure that we too have a sound grasp of what constitutes the *first works*, lest we find ourselves subject to the same error and rebuke as the Church at Ephesus.

CHAPTER 6

FELLOWSHIP:
A PRINCIPLE OF FIRST WORKS

In order to live out the *first works* we need to fully understand and keep in context a very important principle of *first works*, that of **fellowship**, which God instituted since the beginning of time, and which Jesus, before He went to the cross, established as a means to sustain His Church.

The word "fellowship," derived from the Greek word "koinonia" is first mentioned in scripture in the book of Acts:

> And they (the disciples) continued stedfastly in the apostles' doctrine and **fellowship (koinonia)**, and in breaking of bread, and in prayers.
>
> —Acts 2:42
> (emphasis and amplification added)

A study of this Greek word "koinonia" reveals that it contains much deeper nuances than our English word "fellowship" would suggest. Koinonia speaks not only of "association, and community," but also of "communion and joint participation."[10] Furthermore, it conveys the idea of oneness and sharing among those who hold something in common[11]. It is this common ground which unites, builds trust and establishes true fellowship. The concept of koinonia, therefore, transcends self-centeredness, and instead suggests a striving toward those things that would advance the community and its purpose rather than an individual's objective. Fellowship (Koinonia), as God intended, is that unity founded by a common belief in Jesus Christ, which is evidenced among Christians who are knitted together by God's love.

This fellowship to which the believer in Christ is called must mirror that which we see

---

[10] "G2842 - koinōnia - Strong's Greek Lexicon (KJV)." Blue Letter Bible. Web. 13 March, 2017.
[11]Ibid.

among the Godhead. Nothing interrupts the harmony that exists among the Father, the Son and the Holy Spirit of God. So intimately joined are they that the scripture says ". . . The LORD our God is **one** LORD:" (Deuteronomy 6:4b, emphasis added). They are in complete accord with one another, having the same mind and the same purposes, and are equal with one another. There is no competition or strife among them, and they do nothing to hinder that fellowship. Those who are God's children are created in His image and are expected to reflect that oneness. Traits such as hatred, envy, strife, resentment, bitterness and such like are products of the kingdom of darkness.

After the Day of Pentecost[12], when the Holy Spirit came to dwell within the disciples, uniting them to form the body of Christ, the early Church instinctively began to practice this fellowship. Acts chapter two says:

---

[12] See the account in Acts 2:1–4.

And all that believed were together, and had all things common;[45] And sold their possessions and goods, and parted them to all men, as every man had need.[46] And they, continuing daily with one accord in the temple, and breaking bread from house to house, did eat their meat with gladness and singleness of heart,[47] Praising God, and having favour with all the people. And the Lord added to the church daily such as should be saved.

—Acts 2:44–47

The disciples demonstrated true fellowship as they inquired of the needs and concerns of one another and ensured that those needs were met. Selfishness or greed was not a part of their Christianity, but instead **pure brotherly love constantly testified of their covenant with Jesus and with one another.** Christ honored them by strengthening their faith, giving them favor among all men and adding thousands to the Church. Everyone who gladly received the gospel of Jesus Christ and became a part of the family of God adopted this *first works* principle of fellowship as they were taught by faithful apostles. It became a way of life for them.

Listen for a moment to the words of the philosopher, Aristides, as he described the believers in Christ in his letter to the King Hadrian in AD 125:

> "They walk in all humility and kindness, and falsehood is not found among them, and they love one another. They despise not the widow, and grieve not the orphan. He that hath distributeth liberally to him that hath not. If they see a stranger they bring him under their roof, and rejoice over him, as it were their own brother: for they call themselves brethren, not after the flesh, but after the Spirit and in God; but when one of their poor passes away from the world, and any of them see him, then he provides for his burial according to his ability; and if they hear that any of their number is imprisoned or oppressed for the name of their Messiah, all of them

provide for his needs, and if it is possible he may be delivered, they deliver him. And if there is a man among them that is poor and needy, and they have not among them an abundance of necessaries, they fast two or three days that they may supply the needy with their necessary food."

What a powerful testimony! True fellowship was made evident by their actions and, consequently, many who did not know Christ were drawn to Him. Can the Church today afford to neglect this vital principle of the *first works*? Surely not!

Although the term "fellowship" (koinonia) was not expressly mentioned in scripture until after the day of Pentecost, the principle of fellowship is, in fact, one of God's "first things." It was an established part of God's plan for His children even from the very beginning. God created us in His image primarily for intimate love relationship and fellowship with Him first and, subsequently, with one another. Therefore as we love Jesus Christ first, we are able to love one another and do the things that constitute the *first works,* which keeps us in that intimate fellowship with Him and with one another. On the other hand, when we lose our *first love* for Jesus Christ and God the Father, our fellowship with others will inevitably be adversely impacted. Impaired fellowship makes it impossible to maintain *first works.*

Let us take a look at an apt example of this with the first man and woman, Adam and Eve in the Garden of Eden. We have already learned that Adam and Eve had sinned against God and their personal harmony with God was squandered through their fall from *first love.* But beyond that, we see strife and accusation entering into the once peaceable paradise as, almost immediately, Adam began to cast blame on Eve for his broken fellowship with God (Genesis 3:12). Koinonia, that precious, intimate fellowship that they once enjoyed, was no more. It is clear from this account that our fellowship with others as God intended is indeed a reflection of our proper relationship with God. Furthermore, if we consider the account in Genesis chapter four of Adam and Eve's sons, Cain and Abel, we will see a pattern of a progressive loss of fellowship emerging. Let us take a closer look at this Biblical account.

The Bible tells us that both Cain and Abel brought an offering to God but God rejected Cain's offering. Cain gave to God what *he* thought God should accept—the fruit of his own hands—rather than the blood sacrifice which *God* required[13]. God saw this as Cain wanting to exert his own will over God's will. God considered Cain's offering an unacceptable sacrifice and it was for this reason that He did not receive it. Abel, on the other hand, in obedience to God, offered to Him "the firstlings of his flock"

---

[13] When Cain and Abel made their sacrificial offering to God, the requirement of a blood sacrifice had already been established with their parents (Genesis 3:21) and passed down to them; this is why Hebrews 11:4a states:" *By faith Abel offered unto God a more excellent sacrifice than Cain . . ."*

(Genesis 4:4a)—that blood sacrifice which God required. His obedience reflected his love and reverence for God, as he treasured his relationship and fellowship with Him.

Cain's actions clearly revealed his loss of love, faith, and obedience to God, and this left him open to Satan to increase his influence over him. Cain's failure to maintain reverence, respect, and love for God, left him open for Satan's takeover of his heart, mind, and actions. Now under the influence and control of Satan, he began to despise and hate his brother and he ultimately murdered Abel without conscience and with no thought of the consequences of his evil actions.

Satan had succeeded in disconnecting Cain from God—a fall from *first love*—just as he did with his parents. It is obvious that, he too, like his parents, had allowed Satan to whisper lies in his ear. Cain had to learn the painful lessons of disobedience towards God and His word, and face the consequences of expulsion from the presence of God and that place of God's blessings. Cain had unknowingly removed himself from God's covering and had placed himself under a curse . . . to live the life of a wandering vagabond, alone and cut off from God and family. Even the blessing of good crops was lost to him, all as a result of broken fellowship.

> And he said, What hast thou done? the voice of thy brother's blood crieth unto me from the ground. [11] And now art thou cursed from the earth, which hath opened her mouth to receive thy brother's blood from thy hand; [12] When thou tillest the ground, it shall not henceforth yield unto thee her strength; a fugitive and a vagabond shalt thou be in the earth.
>
> —Genesis 4:10–12

By way of correction, God allowed Cain to discover the grave danger of giving up *first love* for God and of breaking that covenant relationship and authentic fellowship with his brother. When Cain realized that he was now no longer under the protection, provision, and favor of God's covering, he had no peace and lamented:

> . . . My punishment is greater than I can bear. [14] Behold, thou hast driven me out this day from the face of the earth; and from thy face shall I be hid; and I shall be a fugitive and a vagabond in the earth; and it shall come to pass, that every one that findeth me shall slay me.
>
> —Genesis 4:13–14

A vital lesson for the Church today

There is much for us to learn from this entire account. But let us focus on one particularly vital lesson on fellowship as seen through God's response to Cain's complaint:

> And the LORD said unto him, Therefore whosoever slayeth Cain, vengeance shall be taken on him sevenfold. And the LORD set a mark upon Cain, lest any finding him should kill him. [16]And Cain went out from the presence of the LORD, and dwelt in the land of Nod, on the east

47

of Eden.

—Genesis 4:15–16

It is important to note that, although Cain had sinned and was out of the will of God and had been judged by God, God would not permit anyone to take it upon himself to kill Cain. God declared that any such person would suffer vengeance seven times more than Cain's punishment. We see here the immeasurable importance of not breaking fellowship one with another, in spite of God's seemingly harsh dealings with a brother or sister.

It is not God's will for anyone to step out of the principle of *first works* to go against a brother who has fallen, and become his judge and executioner. God's judgment of that brother is sufficient. To take it upon ourselves to go against another is to violate the redemptive spirit and nature of God and Jesus Christ. In so doing, we become a supporter of Satan in his entrapment of a brother.

This is a vital lesson for the Church today. If we adopt a position of condemnation, criticism and revenge toward those who fall into sin, instead of attempting to lovingly restore them to fellowship with God and with one another, or instead of committing them to God in humility, then we, who are also fallible, may one day find ourselves facing failure in some form, and facing the judgement of God "seven times over" for we would have violated this element of the *first works*.

Agape (Love), the cornerstone of Fellowship

> A new commandment I give unto you, That ye love one another; as I have loved you, that ye also love one another. [35] **By this shall all men know that ye are my disciples, if ye have love one to another.**
>
> —John 13:34–35 (emphasis added)

All those who are Jesus' disciples are under covenant with Him and with each other to "love one another." This love is agape, God's unconditional love, and it is the glue that keeps His children knitted together in authentic fellowship, one with another. When we fail to love our fallen brother or sister in Christ, it is an indication that we ourselves are fallen for we have failed to keep the commandment of God to love (John 13:34–35). Often times though, we are blinded by Satan to this fact. God does not take sides with Satan and neither should we. God's love for us is paramount even in His judgement. Whenever He deals with His children, no matter how harshly, and regardless of the form it takes, it is never to destroy us in our sin, but rather to teach us the bitter consequences of sin so that we might learn to avoid it. If God deems it fit to punish us, His intention is always reconciliation and redemption so that we might be restored to fellowship with Him and with one another. This is the ultimate purpose of love—God's love and our love—and it is this kind of love, (agape) that spoils Satan's plans and defeats him. Agape, therefore, is the cornerstone of fellowship. It is that which will propel us to do the *first works.*

Without question, that love which fosters true fellowship requires us to act as our "brother's keeper." God expects members of the Body of Christ to strengthen, support, and encourage our brothers and sisters in Christ; to pick them up when they are fallen; to intercede for them when they are weak; and to defend them when they are exposed to the enemy. He expects us to "cover" one another's sins and proceed to restore them; and to desist from pointing the finger of accusation and criticism, with the understanding that we too are subject to failure. These practices are the visible expression of agape, which is the only firm foundation for authentic Christian fellowship.

This kind of love experienced in true Christian fellowship is not dependent on the favorable acceptance of the other party. It loves because love has been cultivated in the heart, in obedience to the Word of God, and is demonstrated by our wholehearted, unselfish care for one another. It loves even if we are the recipients of another's offence or if we may be among those who love less or care less for the well-being of others. Agape, the God kind of love, is the supreme virtue of the Christian. It is a covenant love which "lays down its life," so to speak, putting aside its own agenda to extend mercy and grace to one another for the greater good: the preservation of unity and fellowship in the body of Christ and the advancement of the kingdom of God. It is this love which was expressed by God when He gave His only Son to save us from sin and eternal separation from Him.

Humility in Fellowship

Another necessary requirement in maintaining fellowship is **humility**. Like all other Christian principles, it is a component of agape and it plays a significant part in our doing the *first works*. A lack of humility often bars us from conforming to the Spirit of Christ and hinders genuine fellowship.

According to Strong's Concordance, our English word, "humility" is derived from the

Greek word, *tapeinophrosynē*[14] which is used in the Bible to speak of having a humble opinion of one's self, and of lowliness of mind (neither arrogant nor self-righteous).[15] We must understand, however, that humility is not self-deprecation as some might think, neither is it a mere façade of piety or modesty. Fallen man is well versed in the art of projecting an outward appearance of humility, all the while harboring within his heart evil inclinations such as pride, envy, bitterness and resentment. Humility, rather, is a heart attitude born out of *first love* relationship with Jesus Christ and it is an imperative in carrying out the *first works* principle. Humility (*Tapeinophrosynē*) as used in the Bible is closely associated with another Greek word *diakoneō* which means to serve, or to minister. It points us to the idea of taking care of the need of others; distributing the things necessary to sustain life; or attending to anything

---

[14] "G5012 - tapeinophrosynē - Strong's Greek Lexicon (KJV)." Blue Letter Bible. Web. 13 March, 2017.
[15] Acts 20:19; Ephesians 4:2; Philippians 2:3; Colossians 3:12

that may serve another's interests.[16] *Diakoneō*—
serving others out of a heart of gratitude for all
that Jesus has done and with love for Him and
one another—is a true measure of humility.
Apostle Peter highlighted this vital characteristic
of humility when he urged the Church to "be
**clothed with humility [tie on the servant's
apron]**: for God resisteth the proud, and giveth
grace to the humble."[17]

Jesus endeavored to teach His disciples the
need to practice humility as it cultivates the right
spirit which is needed in doing the *first works*. On
that Passover night before He died, Jesus wanted
to impress upon His disciples that if they were to
remain in Him (connected to Him spiritually)
they must not only serve Him but **they must
serve one another in love and humility**. To
demonstrate this in a graphic and unmistakable
way, He began to wash their feet. The roads of the
cities in those days were unpaved and Jesus and

---

[16] "G1247 - diakoneō - Strong's Greek Lexicon (KJV)." Blue
Letter Bible. Web. 13 March, 2017.
[17] 1 Peter 5:5b (Amplified Bible, emphasis added)

His disciples walked for miles amid the dust of the streets. The customary Jewish tradition at that time was to provide water for one's guests to wash their feet. In some instances, as a mark of honor, the host would have the lowliest slave of the household wash the feet of the guests upon their arrival.[18] That Jesus Christ, their Lord and Master, would humble Himself to assume this menial task was a radical departure from tradition. To the Jewish mind, which esteemed outward cleanliness as a virtue, touching the filthy feet of someone was unthinkable. This extreme act on the part of Jesus was intended therefore to leave an indelible impression on the minds of the disciples. Such a selfless voluntary act of lowering oneself is incorporated in the principle of fellowship.

---

[18] Emil G. Hirsch, Wilhelm Nowack and Solomon Schechter. "Washing of Feet," *The Jewish Encyclopedia* (Online), http://www.jewishencyclopedia.com/articles/6051-feet-washing-of, Accessed March 3, 2017.

It must be noted however, that Jesus never intended that foot washing should become a doctrinal practice to impress Him and the Father with our humility and piety in an effort to win Their favor. He did it purely as a demonstration to His disciples that His divine position as Son of God and His office of Savior and Lord did not exempt Him from His role of servanthood. Likewise, **our calling to represent God to others does not exempt us from being a servant.** On the contrary, it should relentlessly move us to serve our brethren. Such service is a demonstration of the spirit and nature of Christ. It is a practical and visible living out of one's covenant relationship with one another. Let us look a little more intently at what Jesus did that night:

> Now before the feast of the passover, when Jesus knew that his hour was come that he should depart out of this world unto the Father, having loved his own which were in the world, he loved them unto the end. ² And supper being ended,

the devil having now put into the heart of Judas Iscariot, Simon's son, to betray him; ³ Jesus knowing that the Father had given all things into his hands, and that he was come from God, and went to God; ⁴ He riseth from supper, and laid aside his garments; and took a towel, and girded himself. ⁵ After that he poureth water into a bason, and began to wash the disciples' feet, and to wipe them with the towel wherewith he was girded.

—John 13:1–5

Jesus knew that His departure was imminent and He wanted to ensure that His disciples clearly grasped this foundational principle of humility in fellowship, so vital in doing the *first works*. Jesus knew that His disciples, mistakenly believing that He had come to establish His kingdom on earth, were vying among themselves for the highest position. Each estimated himself more worthy than the other, so they argued among themselves as to who was the greatest.[19] In so doing, they disregarded *first love* and *first works* altogether and they began to compete with one another. This competitive spirit threatened to break fellowship and Jesus intervened to put an end to it with this graphic display of humility by washing their feet. His knowledge of His deity did not prevent Him from ministering to the needs of others, preserving fellowship. Jesus understood that if the Christianity that He was about to establish was to survive, Christians must clearly grasp all the principles that hold their covenant relationship in place. Surely, if we are to reflect Christ to the world, the Church today must resolve to always walk in humility to avoid any behaviors or attitudes that impair fellowship.

The Magnitude of Fellowship

By now it should be abundantly clear that, contrary to popular belief, fellowship is much more than just a gathering of Christians for a church service, or for entertainment or fun. It is

---

[19] Mark 9: 33–34; Luke 22:24.

certainly more than a handshake or a hug. It is even more than coming together to do good works or any church related activities. In Biblical terms, fellowship (koinonia) undoubtedly refers to the shared intimacy and oneness that members of the family of God are expected to have because they have been joined to one another through Jesus Christ, in covenant relationship. Fellowship conveys the idea of being so intricately interwoven one with the other that to break that relationship would result in a tearing apart that could potentially damage the whole entity. Such is the importance of fellowship. Christian fellowship, inclusive of our love and humility, is a hallmark of authentic Christianity. It testifies that we are obedient in keeping the principles of our faith and is the undeniable proof to the world that we belong to Christ.

Those who profess to belong to Christ but do not administer agape with a view to keeping and/or restoring broken fellowship with Christ and with one another, their claim to Christianity is not biblical and must be questioned. The apostle John corroborates this:

> In this the children of God are manifest,
> and the children of the devil: whosoever
> doeth not righteousness **is not of God,**
> neither **he that loveth not his brother.**
> [11] For this is the message that ye heard
> from the beginning, that we should love
> one another. [12] Not as Cain, who was of
> that wicked one, and slew his brother.
> And wherefore slew he him? Because his
> own works were evil, and his brother's
> righteous.
>
> —1 John 3:10–12 (emphasis added)

In the above scripture we see that those who belong to Christ and are a part of His Body must give evidence that they are His, that is to say, they love as He loves and possess Christ's redemptive spirit. I must stress here, that **the degree of our love for one another is in fact, an accurate measure of the intensity of our love for God.** If we are not living in fellowship with one another, this is a sure signal that our love for God has diminished, and, unless we hasten to repent and do these *first works,* we will ultimately disqualify ourselves as Christians for we do not reflect the nature of Christ.

Listen to the apostle John as he continues to instruct us about the magnitude of fellowship:

> This then is the message which we have heard of him, and declare unto you, that God is light, and in him is no darkness at all. ⁶ If we say that we have fellowship with him, and walk in darkness, we lie, and do not the truth: ⁷ But **if we walk in the light, as he is in the light, we have fellowship one with another, and the blood of Jesus Christ his Son cleanseth us from all sin.**
>
> —1 John 1:5–7 (emphasis added)

Here again, John alerts us to a vital truth about fellowship, and that is that the cleansing power of the blood of Jesus is active to forgive all our sin as we remain in fellowship one with another. Conversely, he infers that **persistent refusal to**

live in fellowship with one another effectively nullifies the power of the blood of Jesus Christ to render us pure and clean and therefore acceptable to the Father. This is a remarkable and terrifying truth. It matters not what we do for God: whether we tithe, whether we are involved in multiple ministries, whether we feed the poor, or do any such "works." If we do not walk in fellowship, our works would not meet God's requirement for His acceptance. It is like Cain's offering which God did not accept. The magnitude of fellowship with one another is undeniable.

Let us now look at some examples in scripture which show how significant fellowship is to God and why He often times deals harshly with those who are bent on disrupting fellowship among His people. Consider the account in the Book of Numbers, Chapter sixteen, which points us to Korah, one of the Levites assigned to burn incense in the temple of God. This was certainly a privileged position but Korah was not content with his God-given assignment. Instead, he coveted the leadership position of Moses and Aaron. Under the guise of justice, he stirred up others among the Levites and among the congregation, accusing Moses and Aaron of lifting themselves up above the congregation of the Lord. Moses, their leader, was struck with grief, not because his position was threatened, but because he understood that this lust for power would rupture the treasured fellowship that marked the people of God, and he said to Korah:

> Seemeth it but a small thing unto you, that the God of Israel hath separated you from the congregation of Israel, to bring you near to himself to do the service of the tabernacle of the Lord, and to stand before the congregation to minister unto them?
>
> —Numbers 16:9

God ultimately destroyed Korah and those who aligned themselves with him by causing the earth to open up and swallow them all. The account of Korah's uprising is a graphic lesson for us, not just to warn against rebellion against God's appointed leaders, but to vividly caution against sowing any seeds of discord that disrupt the fellowship of the people of God.

Centuries later, the apostle Paul observed similar disruptive jealousies among the Church at Corinth and rebuked them, saying:

> God is faithful, by whom ye were called unto the fellowship of his Son Jesus Christ our Lord. [10] Now I beseech you, brethren, by the name of our Lord Jesus Christ, that ye all speak the same thing, and **that there be no divisions among you; but that ye be perfectly joined together in the same mind and in the same judgment.** [11] For it hath been declared unto me of you, my brethren, by them which are of the house of Chloe, that there are contentions among you. [12] Now this I say, that every one of you saith, I am of Paul; and I of Apollos; and I of Cephas; and I of Christ. [13] **Is Christ divided?** was Paul crucified for you? or were ye

baptized in the name of Paul?

—1 Corinthians 1:9–13 (emphasis added)

In an effort to convey to the Corinthians the inestimable value of remaining united in fellowship and doing the first works, the Holy Spirit impressed upon Paul the analogy of the physical body to describe the function of the Church—the Body of Christ:

> For as the body is one, and hath many members, and all the members of that one body, being many, are one body: so also is Christ. [13] For by one Spirit are we all baptized into one body, whether we be Jews or Gentiles, whether we be bond or free; and have been all made to drink into one Spirit. [14] For the body is not one member, but many.
>
> —1 Corinthians 12:12–14

Like the Church at Ephesus in Revelation chapter two, the church at Corinth was a gifted and active church and may have appeared outwardly to be successful yet Paul upbraided them severely because they had allowed Satan to come in and cause division and strife among them. They had broken fellowship and had laid aside their commitment to that covenant relationship with one another. They had failed to do the *first works.*

Paul pointed out to the Corinthians that the Body of Christ ought not to be divided. He reminded them that behaviors and attitudes that lead to broken fellowship are contrary to the *first works* and are sure signs that they are still carnal, that is, ruled by their previously unredeemed nature[20]. Such behaviors and attitudes are contrary to what God expects of those who are His:

> And I, brethren, could not speak unto you as unto spiritual, but as unto carnal, even as unto babes in Christ. [2]I have fed you with milk, and not with meat: for hitherto

---

[20] For further clarification see: de Bourg, Austin. "The Reality and Conflict of the Dual Nature of the Christian," *What Really is Christianity, Second Edition*. North Charleston: CreateSpace Independent Publishing, 2014. 89-112. Print.

ye were not able to bear it, neither yet now are ye able ^{3} For ye are yet carnal: for whereas there is among you envying, and strife, and divisions, are ye not carnal, and walk as men?

—1 Corinthians 3:1–3

There was much spiritual "meat"—greater revelation of Jesus Christ—that Paul longed to share with the Corinthians but he could not, simply because after so long, they were still not walking in fellowship as there were "envying, and strife, and divisions" among them. If he were to impart greater revelation and knowledge to them, in their carnal state, they would not be able to assimilate it spiritually. More than likely they would become puffed up because their hearts were not prepared to receive such revelation with humility.

God will expel from His Kingdom those who sow seeds of discord among His people; those who harbor envy or unforgiveness and who altogether violate covenant relationship . . .

regardless of their status in the church. He gives us ample opportunity to repent, but if we continue to engage in corrupting those whose hearts are easily swayed, enticing them to join us in gossip or slander, or in any way cause the ill-will of others, we are violating the principle of fellowship and failing to do the first works. In so doing, we are guilty before God. This practice may be widespread in the Church today, and as such, it might appear justifiable, but in the eyes of Christ, those who practice such things could face expulsion from His Church since such actions oppose the principle of first works and thereby open the door for Satan to come to affect the proper functioning of the Church. The words of Solomon in the Book of Proverbs clearly underscore those traits and actions that God hates because they shatter fellowship among His children:

> These six things doth the Lord **hate**: yea, seven are an abomination unto him: [17] **A proud look, a lying tongue, and hands that shed innocent blood,** [18] An heart

that deviseth wicked imaginations, feet
that be swift in running to mischief,
[19] A false witness that speaketh lies, and
he that soweth discord among
brethren.

—Proverbs 6:16–19 (emphasis added)

Let me remind you that God did not only
judge Korah, Abiram and Dathan, the leaders of
the rebellion against Moses, but all those who
stubbornly followed their wicked counsel. Jesus
Christ and God the Father hold each of us
responsible for allowing Satan to deceive us and
derail us from Their purpose which is given to us
in the Word of God. Thus, in Korah's rebellion
against Moses, two hundred and fifty of the
members of the council also perished.
Furthermore, their families were also destroyed,
for both God's blessings and curses upon His
people are passed on to their seed.

Know this! Fellowship among God's
people is a treasure and a delight to God and
when we do anything to impede or destroy this

fellowship among His people, we can be sure that we, and often our families, will pay a heavy price. God is constant in all His ways. Will He judge Cain, Korah and his trouble-making supporters for marring fellowship among His children and not judge us today? Certainly not! God is unyielding in this matter.

CHAPTER 7

BREAKING OF BREAD

O n the night before Jesus died, He instituted a vital ordinance, one that, if practiced as Jesus intended, will keep His Church united in fellowship (koinonia), secure in their *first love* for Him and doing the *first works* with one another. This ordinance is the **'Breaking of Bread'** and it holds great significance for the Body of Christ.

The term *'Breaking of Bread'* is often used interchangeably with the terms, "communion" or "the Lord's Supper" or "the Lord's table" or "the cup of the Lord." Regardless of which term we use, it is critical to our understanding of the *first works* that we grasp the significance of what Jesus intended when He instituted this practice. Let us look more closely at what transpired on that night.

Jesus and His disciples had gathered together to celebrate the feast of the Passover, a Jewish tradition where family and loved ones gathered together to share a special love meal in remembrance of the Jews' triumphant deliverance out of bondage in Egypt. It was a time of togetherness and oneness, a sharing of love and affection, as they broke and ate of one loaf of bread and drank out of one cup as only close families do. As they ate, they would reflect on the love, faithfulness, mercy, wisdom and power of God and would rehearse the events of that memorable first Passover when God supernaturally delivered their people from slavery in Egypt. They would recall how God had instructed their forefathers to slay a lamb and smear its blood on the lintels and doorposts of their homes as a sacrifice offered, a substitute— one life laid down to redeem another. God had promised the Jews that, if they obeyed His instruction, the angel of death (His final judgement on the land of Egypt and its inhabitants) would "pass over" their homes. Just as God had further instructed their forefathers to partake of the slain lamb with their families (Exodus 12), they too, would kill, roast and eat a lamb in obedience to God's command to pass on the ordinance of "The Lord's Passover" from generation to generation. This was to be a reminder of how their faith in God and in the integrity of His word brought about their miraculous salvation from death, heralding their freedom from the bondage of slavery.

It was no coincidence that Jesus chose this particular time of the Passover to have this important last supper with His disciples. Jesus knew that the time was at hand for Him to fulfill the Old Testament prophecy which foretold that He would be sacrificed for the sins of mankind. The Passover was indeed, of paramount significance. You see, that Passover lamb centuries ago was but a foreshadowing of the perfect Lamb of God—Jesus Christ—who was about to lay down His life to redeem all of mankind from the curse of sin and eternal death. Jesus was about to become that ultimate Passover Lamb! So it was, that on this night in question

Jesus began the meal by saying to His disciples, "With desire I have desired to eat this passover with you before I suffer . . ." (Luke 22:15). These words gave expression of the highest level of longing, passion, and enthusiasm that burned in Jesus' heart because what He was about to do would bring them into a lasting covenant relationship with Himself. Jesus then took the customary bread, pierced with holes and marked with stripes, traditionally called the "bread of affliction,"[21] broke it, and said to His disciples "this is my body which is given for you" (Luke 22:19). Jesus was alluding to the fact that very soon, His own body would become as this "bread of affliction," pierced and bruised for the sake of all and ultimately slain on behalf of all mankind. Jesus then lifted the cup of wine which would have traditionally been drunk in remembrance of the blood of the lamb sacrificed that first Passover. On this occasion however, Jesus declared that the wine represented the blood by which the new covenant that He was about to

---

[21] Deuteronomy 16:3

establish would be ratified—**His own blood** which would be poured out for many for the forgiveness of sin (Luke 22:19–20).

Jesus intentionally used the occasion of the Passover family gathering to put in place a **new** ordinance, one that would be passed on from generation to generation among members of a **new** family, **the family of God** (the ones who will accept Jesus' sacrifice and who would forsake all to follow Him and live in accordance with the new covenant that He was about to establish). This ordinance is the *Breaking of Bread or Communion* which is intended as a love feast . . . a united expression of the believers' love for God and for one another as one family of God, one Body of Christ.

As His departure from this earth was imminent, Jesus was eager to institute this ordinance which, if practiced correctly, would solidify His disciples' love for Him and for one another, maintain unity among them and guide the living-out of their faith in the way that would please both Him and the Father. It would keep the door shut so that Satan and his forces would not be able to come among them and deceive and divide His Church. Furthermore, it would keep the memory of Him alive in their hearts until that day when He would once again raise the cup and drink together with them in Heaven.

> For I say unto you, I will not any more eat thereof, until it be fulfilled in the kingdom of God... [18] For I say unto you, I will not drink of the fruit of the vine, until the kingdom of God shall come.
>
> —Luke 22:16, 18

It is imperative that we grasp the significance that this ordinance holds to Christians, the Body of Christ. Every time we partake of the *Breaking of Bread* we rekindle in our hearts the memory of Christ's sacrifice which redeemed us from the curse of sin, and death— eternal separation from God; a sacrifice which brought us into the family of God and into that covenant love relationship with Jesus which was ratified by God in Heaven through His acceptance of Christ's sinless blood.

Additionally, just as the meal in ancient covenants was a reminder of the terms and conditions of that covenant, so too, as we break bread together we are reminded of the terms and conditions of the covenant that Jesus instituted. These are the duties and responsibilities of the members of the Body of Christ to one another and to Christ Himself. Thus this ordinance provides us with an opportunity to keep the covenant bond of love and fellowship one with another. This is what Jesus refers to as *first works*.

The **Breaking of Bread is, therefore, an avenue through which we express our *first love* for Jesus Christ, promote fellowship and do the *first works* principle of upholding one another in the Christian faith.** In all our acts we mirror the love of Christ and constantly strive to be in harmony and unity with one another, administering agape (God's love), respecting, caring for, and defending one another, as the word of God dictates:

> That there should be no schism in the body; but that the members should have the same care one for another.[26] And whether one member suffer, all the members suffer with it; or one member be honoured, all the members rejoice with it.
>
> —1 Corinthians 12:25–26

The intimacy and fellowship which the Father has determined for the Body of believers to have with His Son and with one another is therefore reinforced at the table of the Lord. Wherever this love meal is executed in the way that Christ has prescribed, He is present to ensure that we reap the blessings of covenant: spiritual and physical wellness whereby we are able to effectively carry on the work of the kingdom of God. When we uphold the terms of our covenant with Him and with one another, Christ confirms the authority He has given us through His Name.

The ordinance of *Breaking of Bread,* which Jesus instituted on the night before He died, is indeed crucial to the unity, health, power, and success of the Church while it is on the earth. However, if we focus only on the bread and wine giving it some meaning which Christ did not intend; or, if we partake of it as a mere ritual; or if we think that it would remove sins as many are led to believe, we miss the intended purpose of this fundamental and critical ordinance. Unless we live out that covenant relationship, loving as Christ loves in authentic fellowship with all members of the Body of Christ, it will profit us nothing and, indeed it can actually be injurious to us as the apostle Paul reveals!

Carelessly Partaking of Communion

The *breaking of bread (communion)* is strictly for the members of the body of Christ—those who have experienced the new birth[22]. It is

---

[22] John 3:3–6; For further information see: de Bourg, Austin. "Christ's Christianity," *What Really is Christianity, Second Edition.* North Charleston: CreateSpace Independent Publishing, 2014. 32-38. Print.

a dangerous practice to ignorantly partake of this ordinance if we have not had this new birth experience. Additionally, to the Christian who is a part of the body of Christ and understands the purpose for the communion, to partake when you are not in conformity to the word and will of God, you are guilty of "trampling" on the body of Christ, so to speak.

The apostle Paul, having grasped the significance of this, chided the Christians at Corinth for wrongly partaking of the *breaking of bread*. He rebuked them for coming together with the wrong condition of heart that contradicted covenant relationship and fellowship:

> Now in this that I declare unto you I praise you not, that ye come together not for the better, but for the worse. [18] For first of all, when ye come together in the church, I hear that there be divisions among you; and I partly believe it. [19] For there must be also heresies among you, that they which are approved may be

made manifest among you.

—1 Corinthians 11:17–19

Paul then cautioned them that this was the wrong approach to partaking of the Lord's Supper, for it altogether negated the intentions for communion:

> When ye come together therefore into one place, this is not to eat the Lord's supper. [21] For in eating every one taketh before other his own supper: and one is hungry, and another is drunken. [22] What? have ye not houses to eat and to drink in? or despise ye the church of God, and shame them that have not? what shall I say to you? shall I praise you in this? I praise you not.
>
> —1 Corinthians 11:20–22

So vital was this ordinance to Jesus that He was careful to specifically instruct Paul to teach others of its significance:

For I have received of the Lord that which also I delivered unto you, that the Lord Jesus the same night in which he was betrayed took bread: [24] And when he had given thanks, he brake it, and said, Take, eat: this is my body, which is broken for you: this do in remembrance of me. [25] After the same manner also he took the cup, when he had supped, saying, this cup is the new testament in my blood: this do ye, as oft as ye drink it, in remembrance of me. [26] For as often as ye eat this bread, and drink this cup, ye do shew the Lord's death till he come.

—1 Corinthians 11:23–26

(emphasis added)

One can almost hear Paul's stern admonishment to the Christians at Corinth: that they were never to partake of the communion lightly, for in doing so, they disrespected and dishonored the sacrifice of Jesus Christ and thereby, heaped damnation onto themselves:

Wherefore whosoever shall eat this bread, and drink this cup of the Lord, unworthily, shall be guilty of the body and blood of the Lord. [28] But let a man examine himself, and so let him eat of that bread, and drink of that cup. [29] **For he that eateth and drinketh unworthily, eateth and drinketh damnation to himself, not discerning the Lord's body. [30] For this cause many are weak and sickly among you, and many sleep [die].**

—1 Corinthians 11:27–30
(emphasis and amplification added)

Paul continued to appeal to the Christians at Corinth to "judge themselves" to ensure that they were living in their covenant relationship with Jesus Christ and with one another. If they were to partake of the Lord's Table without having examined themselves in this specific regard, they would forfeit their covenant blessings and face the same consequences as those who are not members of the body of Christ: physical weakness, sickness, or premature death.

For if we would **judge ourselves,** we should not be judged. [32] But when we are judged, we are chastened of the Lord, that we **should not be condemned with the world.** [33] Wherefore, my brethren, when ye come together to eat, tarry one for another. [34] And if any man hunger, let him eat at home; **that ye come not together unto condemnation.** And the rest will I set in order when I come.

—1 Corinthians 11:31–34

(emphasis added)

A study of Paul's epistles to the church at Corinth reveals that they were living like the world with division, boasting, envy and such like among them, and not according to the *first works* principle, yet they were taking part in the *breaking of bread.*

Paul drove his point home when he said to them that their divisive behaviors were contrary to Christ and were, in fact, representative of Satan and His kingdom of darkness. He admonished them, saying:

> Ye cannot drink of the cup of the Lord,
> and the cup of devils: ye cannot be
> partakers of the Lord's Table, and of the
> table of devils:
>
> —1 Corinthians 10:21

The apostle urged them to abandon their selfish agendas and to do the first works, that is, to serve one another in covenant love and faithfulness.

Allow me to again underscore the awful price for violating covenant. The Bible tells us, in Luke 22:5, that although Judas Iscariot professed to be in relationship with Jesus Christ as his Lord, he had entered into covenant with the chief priests to betray Jesus, all out of misplaced personal ambition. By doing so, he dishonored covenant with Jesus and, by extension, with his fellow disciples. At the last supper, knowing what was in Judas' heart, Jesus offered him the bread as a gesture of brotherly love and fellowship, but because he had so deeply joined himself to those who were in league with Satan to kill Jesus, Satan's hold upon him was so strong that he could not accept it. The offering of the sop was Jesus offering Judas the opportunity to repent and come back into covenant relationship. When Judas rejected it, he officially abandoned his salvation, turned his back on Jesus Christ, his brethren and the Christian faith, to openly join forces with Satan against Jesus. From Judas' experience we see what Satan does to us when he is finished using us to do his bidding . . . Judas hanged himself. This was his unexpected outcome for breaking covenant with Jesus Christ and the family of God.

Believers in every generation and every Church age risk losing their souls to Satan when, in their hearts and practices, they shift from the word of God and compromise truth. In so doing, they fail to maintain *first love* for Jesus Christ and they fail to do the *first works*. When we violate our covenant relationship with Jesus Christ and with one another, we defile the table of the Lord and let Satan in. Satan comes in only to steal, kill and destroy (John 10:10). However, the Church of Jesus Christ can defeat him when we maintain *first love* for Jesus Christ and do the *first works.* This vital ordinance of *Breaking bread* which Jesus instituted must therefore be centered on fellowship with Jesus Christ and with one another, and this fellowship must be based on our genuine love for one another. As we practice this ordinance in this manner, it will keep our hearts in the right condition at all times.

CHAPTER 8

COVENANT RELATIONSHIP

I t should be clear by now, that the power of *first love* and *first works* is indeed undeniable. These two intricately intertwined relationships are based on the lasting strength of **covenant** and that is what makes them so powerful. It is important therefore, to have a clear understanding of what it means to enter into covenant with another as it will undoubtedly help us to gain further insight into why Jesus responds as He does to those who leave their first love and who fail to do the first works.

According to Baker's Evangelical Dictionary of Biblical Theology, the term "covenant" is of Latin origin—con venire—and refers to "a coming together," a joining as it were, to another, essentially relinquishing independent living and operating, for all intents and purposes, as a single unified body, bound together forever.

Understanding the ancient rite of covenanting therefore provides further insights into this *first love* relationship which God wants with us, and what it means to walk in covenant relationship with Jesus and with one another.

The blood covenant was the most binding of all ancient covenants. It was entered into as a sacred, solemn, and high symbolic ceremony. During this ceremony, the terms of the covenant were explicitly stated and confirmed by an oath. This oath was further ratified by the shedding of the blood of an animal.[23] It is important to note that not only did these promises, stipulations, privileges, and responsibilities of ancient covenants apply to the two immediate parties, but they were also extended to include the seed or progeny of each party from generation to generation. In this way, the newly formed entity was perpetuated and its power was preserved.

---

[23] Van Groningen, Gerard. "Covenant." Baker's Evangelical Dictionary of Biblical Theology, edited by Walter A. Elwell, Baker Books, 1996. *Bible Study Tools Online*, http://www.biblestudytools.com/dictionaries/bakers-evangelical-dictionary/

Author Ken Kessler, in his book *Understanding Your Inheritance in Christ* provides historical data on "ancient-covenant making." According to Kessler, at the start of the ceremony the two contracting parties or their representatives would exchange robes and belts. Each robe represented the person himself, both his identity and his authority. Through the exchange of the belts which held their weapons they were pledging protection to each other and to each other's families. This exchange of robes and belts symbolized an offering of one's life, so to speak, to one's covenant partner who then had the authority to use his name to secure protection, provision and peace.

In some practices, the two parties would cut their palms and clasp each other by the hand so that the blood of both parties would mingle together, becoming "one blood," indistinct from each other and having, in that sense, one identity. The scar that resulted from the cut would be the visible proof of that blood covenant. If an enemy would attempt to attack one of the parties, that

91

person would "plead the blood," calling the enemy's attention to the scar and thereby letting him know that if he engaged in warfare with one party, he was, in essence, also confronting that person's covenant partner. Where the enemy saw evidence of a blood covenant, therefore, he would be more likely to retreat. The scar would also be a clear reminder to each party of his covenant responsibilities.

Additionally, the covenant parties would often exchange names, each taking a part of the other person's name and incorporating it into their own. This, according to Kessler, was more than just an external symbol, it implied the exchange of character, reputation and authority, again signifying oneness. Finally, the terms of the covenant stipulated that everything that belonged to one party essentially "belonged" to the other, including all of one's assets as well as one's debts.[24]

---

[24] Kessler, Ken. "Steps of Ancient-Covenant Making," *Understanding Your Inheritance in Christ.* Marietta: Restoration Times Publications, 2004. Print.

In the same way, when Jesus Christ established the new covenant with His followers, which was ratified by His own blood, He was giving His followers the assurance that they were no unified as One Body with Him forever. All that belongs to Him would now be theirs. He would provide for them and defend them against all attacks. All who enter into this new covenant with Jesus would have the right to invoke the authority which is in the blood of Jesus and to use His name to secure protection, provision and peace.

The Bible is replete with both allusions to and clear mention of covenant throughout the Old Testament. Two of the most significant examples are the Abrahamic covenant (Genesis 12:1–3 & Genesis 15) and the Mosaic covenant (Exodus 19–24). Another clear illustration of covenant relationship is that which was established between David and Jonathan and documented in the Book of Samuel. As we take a brief look at this account we will see how covenant underpins both *first love* and the *first works.*

Jonathan, King Saul's son, loved David as a brother and they entered into covenant with each other, exchanging robes and belts as was the practice in covenant ritual (1 Samuel 18:1–4). The Bible tells us in 1 Samuel 18:5–16, that King Saul was embittered by the people's love for David and was so envious of his military successes that he sought to have him killed. David recognized Saul's increasingly crazed determination to destroy him and fled for his life. Although Jonathan could not initially believe that his father was bent on killing David, once he confirmed David's fears, Jonathan met secretly with David and they reaffirmed their solemn covenant. One would expect that being next in line for the kingship, Jonathan would be only too happy to accommodate his father's wish for David to be killed. Instead, Jonathan remained faithful to his covenant with David and put his own life on the line to protect him from Saul's evil intentions having recognized that David was indeed **God's** chosen king. After Jonathan's death and David's ascension to the throne, David sought for any of Jonathan's children so that he might honor his generational covenant with Jonathan. David was told of Mephibosheth, Jonathan's lame son. Many around King David considered Mephibosheth to be either useless to David or a threat to him but David placed a ring and a robe on Mephibosheth, thereby incorporating him into the royal household as a member of his own family. By his actions, David was pledging to care for Jonathan's son and to protect him just as Jonathan would have, had he lived.

As powerful as the covenants in the Old Testament were however, they were but a shadow of the greatest of all covenants . . . the new covenant which Jesus Christ established with those who accept His offer of salvation.

The New Covenant

God has extended an offer to all of mankind to enter into covenant with Him and, thereby, to be restored to oneness and fellowship with Him. The choice to accept or reject God's astounding offer and the terms of that offer is ours. God assumed the roles of both covenant parties to do for man what man could not do for himself. Jesus Christ, the second Person of the Trinity of God, humbled Himself by laying aside His deity and taking on the lowly form of man. As a man He represented all of mankind and, as Son of God, He represented the Godhead.[25]

This new covenant was a blood covenant, ratified by the shed blood of Jesus Christ, the Lamb of God, Who was slain and Whose blood was shed to seal the covenant. The Bible uses several metaphors to describe this binding union between Christ and His disciples. Those who accept Jesus as their only Savior and Lord enter into a *first love* relationship with Him, one that is so intimate that they are considered to be "*in Christ*." They become so deeply connected to Jesus when they accept His offer of salvation that

---

[25] For deeper understanding of this, see: de Bourg, Austin. "Jesus, Son of God–Son of Man," *Insights to the Mystery of the Trinity (Second Edition)*. North Charleston: CreateSpace Independent Publishing, 2014. 85-91. Print.

they are also described as being "members of the Body of Christ," vitally united with Him in integral relationship, now belonging to the family of God, joined in fellowship with Him. God places incomparable worth on this covenant relationship because it cost His Son His very life and because it satisfies the ageless longing of the Father's heart to be reconciled to fellowship with mankind.

In keeping with the establishment of covenant, Jesus took all of man's liabilities upon Himself and extends in their stead all that belongs to Him (Isaiah 53:5). He took upon Himself our robe of unrighteousness and offers to clothe us with His robe of righteousness. He undertook to pay the penalty for our sin, that is, death (Romans 6:23) and offers instead eternal life. Every heavenly blessing becomes ours when we enter into this remarkable covenant with the Son of God and share in His inheritance (Ephesians 1:3). Jesus Christ, the Son of God, also extends to us, His covenant partners, the guarantee of divine provision as well as protection against Satan, our common enemy. The scars that He bears are evidence of that covenant and are a reminder of His enduring love for us. As we remain "in Christ," cleaving to Him in covenant intimacy— that *first love* relationship—and keeping the terms of that blood covenant—doing the *first works*— when Satan, the enemy of our souls, would come to attack us we can then, with confidence invoke or "plead the blood" of Christ, that is to say we cite our mighty blood covenant with Jesus Christ. Where Satan sees **evidence of that blood covenant**, he will retreat, knowing that our covenant partner is none other than Jesus Christ who has pledged to be our shield and defense.

The Holy Spirit, the Word of God and the blood of Jesus Christ are the witnesses of our covenant with Christ and these three (1 John 5:8), being in constant agreement with one another, will judge whether or not the terms of the covenant are being adhered to . . . whether or not we are doing the first works.

CHAPTER 9

CONCLUSION

I t is clear from what has been revealed in this book that members of the body of Christ must be cognizant of the fact that we cannot survive without one another. God, in His divine wisdom, has so arranged the Body of Christ so that we all have need of others in one capacity or another. He has not given to any one person or to any one assembly all the gifts, talents and resources that are necessary for the full functioning of His Body. What is even more remarkable is that He has arranged it so that the parts of the Body that we, in our natural finite thinking, might consider of less value are, in His sight, of great honor.

> And the eye cannot say unto the hand, I have no need of thee: nor again the head to the feet, I have no need of you. [22] Nay, much more those members of the body, which seem to be more feeble, are

necessary: [23] And those members of the body, which we think to be less honourable, upon these we bestow more abundant honour; and our uncomely parts have more abundant comeliness. [24] For our comely parts have no need:

—1 Corinthians 12:21–24a

God has ordered the Body of Christ in such a way that the members must remain joined together in covenant relationship with one another in order to reap the full personal and corporate blessings of our inheritance in Christ:

. . . but God hath tempered the body together, having given more abundant honour to that part which lacked. [25] That there should be no schism in the body; but that the members should have the same care one for another. [26] And whether one member suffer, all the members suffer with it; or one member be honoured, all the members rejoice with it.

—1 Corinthians 12:24b–26

Each part of the Body will find its greatest fulfillment as it functions in that place in which God has set it and in united covenant relationship with other members of Christ's Body, committed above all to serve the interest of the entire Body for the glory of Jesus Christ.

> If the foot shall say, Because I am not the hand, I am not of the body; is it therefore not of the body? [16] And if the ear shall say, Because I am not the eye, I am not of the body; is it therefore not of the body? [17] If the whole body were an eye, where were the hearing? If the whole were hearing, where were the smelling? [18] But now hath God set the members every one of them in the body, as it hath pleased him. [19] And if they were all one member, where were the body? [20] But now are they many members, yet but one body. [21] And the eye cannot say unto the hand, I have no need of thee: nor again the head to the feet, I have no need of you.
>
> —1 Corinthians 12:15–21

Surely God will not tolerate anyone who erects walls of division within the Body of His Son in violation of the principles of *first love* and *first works.* God calls every member to edify, build up, and support the other members using the talents and resources which He has given to them so that the Body of Christ is nurtured and flourishes. The Body of Christ thereby becomes a testimony to those who do not yet know Christ.

All who have accepted God's offer of salvation through Jesus Christ and are born again by the Spirit of God have been reconciled to God and make up this spiritual Body of Christ. And God has ordained that as the Body of Christ unites in covenant love for Jesus Christ and for one another, demonstrating that love as one family of God, the world will know that Jesus Christ is the only Savior and Redeemer of mankind and will be drawn to Him. The responsibility of all those who belong to Jesus is to cultivate that love by maintaining *first love* and by doing the *first works.* In so doing, we will be that illumination so desperately needed to this dark world.

I hope that it is abundantly clear to you that from Genesis to Revelation the scriptures urge us toward doing the first works—toward an unbreakable commitment to be our brother's keeper, to serve one another in love and humility, and to do all in our power to preserve the unity of the Body of Christ. This is the only evidence of our claim to be children of God and the most convincing evidence of our love for Him. Nothing else testifies to the world that we are indeed the people of God . . . not our good deeds, not our gifts . . . nothing but doing the *first works*.

It is my earnest prayer that the Church today would take a sober look at itself in view of this insight and hearken to the words of Jesus Christ, lest we too find ourselves in that dreadful position for all eternity:

> **Nevertheless I have somewhat against thee, because thou hast left thy first love.** [5] **Remember therefore from**

whence thou art fallen, and repent, and do the first works; or else I will come unto thee quickly, and will remove thy candlestick out of his place, except thou repent.

—Revelation 2:4–5 (emphasis added)

This book is the first in a seven-part series on Jesus Christ's Letters To The Seven Churches in the Book of Revelation.

ABOUT THE AUTHOR

Austin J. de Bourg is an accomplished Minister of Jesus Christ and Christian Author.

Through His intimacy with the Trinity, he has received the revelation contained in his books, which include *What Really is Christianity, Misplaced Righteousness, Insights into the Mystery of the Trinity, Working the Harvest, and Know the Truth (Volumes I-IV).*

Austin is a true pioneer. In 1980, he founded and began pastoring the Trinidad Christian Center, the first Independent, Evangelical, Full-Gospel church in the nation of Trinidad and Tobago, which started with a revival that lasted five years, after which over 300 independent churches emerged.

In his over 40 years of effective ministry, he has also established humanitarian projects in rural areas of impoverished countries where food is scarce and founded the Austin de Bourg Foundation for Human Advancement (ADFHA). He has earned a Doctorate in Theology (Th.D.) and has been conferred with four Honorary Doctorates, including the Doctor of Divinity (D.D.) and Doctor of Pastoral Counselling (DPC), and he holds the designation: Christian Certified Chaplain, (C.C.C.) for USA, Canada and Mexico. He also founded Apostolic Renewal Ministries (ARM), aimed at rekindling the apostolic spirit and ministry in the Church.

By every biblical definition, his life and ministry demonstrate the nature and characteristics of true apostolic ministry. Many consider him a father in the faith, and God has sent him to many nations of the world to equip, train, and empower ministers. He has conducted ministerial training in Africa, India, Haiti, Jamaica, Canada, and the USA and has mentored some in Austria and the Ukraine. He continues to affect lives and bring change wherever the Lord sends him.

He is currently working on other books.

OTHER BOOKS BY AUSTIN DE BOURG:

---※---

What Really is Christianity

This book is a wakeup call to slumbering Christians. It focuses on Christianity from God's perspective and reveals the honorable role God has ordained for Christians in His plan for mankind. It takes a look at Christianity, from an aspect rarely considered in modern times, revealing truths from the Word of God on the supernatural birthright and heritage of Christians and Christianity, and answering questions on the seldom taught doctrine of the reality of man's dual nature. It deals with the misconceptions of Christianity citing the dangers of replacing 'relationship with God' with religion. It not only diagnoses the present malady of Christianity, but prescribes the corrective treatment that would bring Christians and Christianity back on the course designed by Jesus Christ.

Misplaced Righteousness

There is a multiplicity of interpretations of the biblical doctrine of righteousness by the many brands of the Christian faith. Each brand presents its particular interpretation with conviction that theirs is right and the others are wrong. *How then can we know what is true righteousness?*

This book enlightens the reader, from the Word of God, on what God's righteousness is and how it differs from what man calls righteousness. It shows how to attain God's righteousness by applying God's formula. It exposes the error and dangers of replacing God's righteousness with man's righteousness.

Man's righteousness is not God's righteousness. Discover the difference in this book.

Insights into the Mystery of the Trinity

"Why would the Almighty God need a Son and a Holy Spirit? Is He lacking in Himself?"

"How could Jesus Christ be God and Man at the same time?"

"Why would such a good and perfect God make such a bad devil?"

These questions and more are answered in this book overflowing with revelation regarding the Trinity, Jesus Christ and Christianity. It takes the reader from eternity to Pentecost and beyond to unfold the saga of the Trinity's quest to restore man from his fallen state back into relationship, fellowship, and dialogue with God. As you read, you will discover priceless treasures that were kept secret by God . . . until now.

Know The Truth

Know the Truth is a four-volume series which addresses wrong Christian teachings on four fundamental doctrines: Saints, Communion, The Church, and Praying versus Saying Prayers.

If we think wrong we will believe wrong and we will act wrong

This is the premise upon which author Austin de Bourg makes his compelling case to get back to the simplicity and authenticity of Biblical Truths. According to Dr. de Bourg:

Truth is truth and error is error, and God alone defines what constitutes truth.

In these volumes the author applies God's method of interpreting doctrine, as given in His word, to correct the errors which for centuries have been presented as truth and embraced by many. The revelation contained in these books is presented with clarity and simplicity and as such, they are a vital resource for anyone who desires truth.

Working the Harvest

Success, victory, and rewards await those who would bring in the harvest. This book brings the reader back in focus with the true spirit and purpose of Christianity. It highlights the biblical formula for success and reveals how to come into the hundred-fold blessings, which include divine favor, divine health, divine provision, divine protection, and freedom from satanic oppression.

AUTHOR'S CONTACT INFORMATION

Apostolic Renewal Ministries
Phone: (868) 633 4037
Email: arm@arm-tcc.org
Website: www.arm-tcc.org

Trinidad Christian Center
Phone: (868) 637 5221
Email: tcc@tcc1980.org
Website: www.tcc1980.org

Made in the USA
Columbia, SC
15 August 2017